PAGC Third Level Services

PRINCE ALBERT GRAND COUNCIL

FULFILLING THE VISION OF TREATY RIGHTS

Compiled by Edward Mirasty, PhD (ABD) and Vincent Brittain, EdD (ABD)

BIG MOOSE PUBLISHING

Copyright 2024 Prince Albert Grand Council. All rights reserved.

Published by:
Big Moose Publishing
234 Pohorecky Street
Saskatoon, SK S7W 0J3
www.bigmoosepublishing.com

All rights reserved. No part of this book may be used or reproduced by any means, graphic, electronic, or mechanical, including photocopying, recording, taping or by any information storage retrieval system without the written permission of the author(s) except in the case of brief quotations embodied in critical articles and reviews.

Because of the dynamic nature of the Internet, any web addresses or links contained in this book may have changed since publication and may no longer be valid. The views expressed in this work are solely those of the author and do not necessarily reflect the views of the publisher, and the publisher hereby disclaims any responsibility for them. The publisher has been informed by the author(s) that they have been given permission to publish all information and images in this book and takes no responsibility for any discrepancy.

ISBN: 978-1-989840-75-7
Big Moose Publishing 08/2024

CONTENTS

Dedication 5

Prince Albert Indian Residential School History 1947-1997 6

Chronology of Prince Albert Grand Council 7

PAGC Numbered Treaties 16

Treaty Timeline 18

PAGC Convention Act 20

Prince Albert Grand Council Organizational Chart 21

Prince Albert Grand Council Executive 22

Prince Albert Grand Council Senators 26

Prince Albert Grand Council Women's Commission 27

Senior Management 28

Prince Albert Grand Council Program Managers and Directors 32

Agriculture 33

Child Care & Education Centre 34

Education Department 36

Forestry and Emergency Protective Services 38

Health and Social Development 40

Housing and Technical Services 42

Human Resources 45

Information Technology 46

Justice Unit 47

Men's Spiritual Healing Lodge 49

Spruce Lodge Boarding Home	50
Urban Services	51
Prince Albert Grand Council Communities	52
Wahpeton Dakota Nation	53
Shoal Lake Cree Nation	54
Sturgeon Lake First Nation	55
Black Lake Denēsuline First Nation	56
Lac La Ronge Indian Band	57
Peter Ballantyne Cree Nation	58
Cumberland House Cree Nation	59
Fond du Lac Denēsuline First Nation	60
James Smith Cree Nation	61
Montreal Lake Cree Nation	62
Hatchet Lake Denēsuline First Nation	63
Red Earth Cree Nation	64
Help Line for Residential School Survivors	65
Special Thanks	66
Bibliography	67

DEDICATION

Ron Michel
Dec 6th, 1951 - Jan 25th, 2021

"*There are some leaders who simply command respect, not only because they display a determined, fierce and confident attitude in their cause...they command respect because those qualities are driven by compassion and a deep love for the people.*" Senator Michel was one of those leaders. He never showed anger in the way that many of us do. Michel met challenges with kindness, respect and compassion. Michel was also a strong advocate for First Nations children.

Robert Ronald Michel "Ron" was born on Thursday, December 6, 1951, in Sandy Bay, SK, and passed away on Monday, January 25, 2021, in Prince Albert, SK, at the age of 69 years.

For more than 30 years, Ron Michel served in leadership as Chief of the Peter Ballantyne Cree Nation, then Grand Chief of the Prince Albert Grand Council. The PAGC dedicates this book to him.

Chief Ron Michel with PAGC Leadership 1995

Grand Chief Ron Michel as coach of PAGC Chiefs Hockey Team

Grand Chief Ron Michel with Minister Ralph Goodale

Ron Michel at Inaugral PAGC Sponsored Remembrance Day

Grand Chief Ron Michel with Ken Dryden 2008

Chief Ron Michel with Prime Minister Jean Chretien 1996

PRINCE ALBERT INDIAN RESIDENTIAL SCHOOL HISTORY 1947-1997

As one author notes, "In order to escape accountability for his crimes, the perpetrator does everything in his power to promote forgetting." (Herman, 1997: 8). In Canada, for instance the narrative of colonial violence associated with the residential school era was left out of the national story for a number of decades. (Cote-Meek, 2018, p. 32)

CHRONOLOGY OF PRINCE ALBERT GRAND COUNCIL

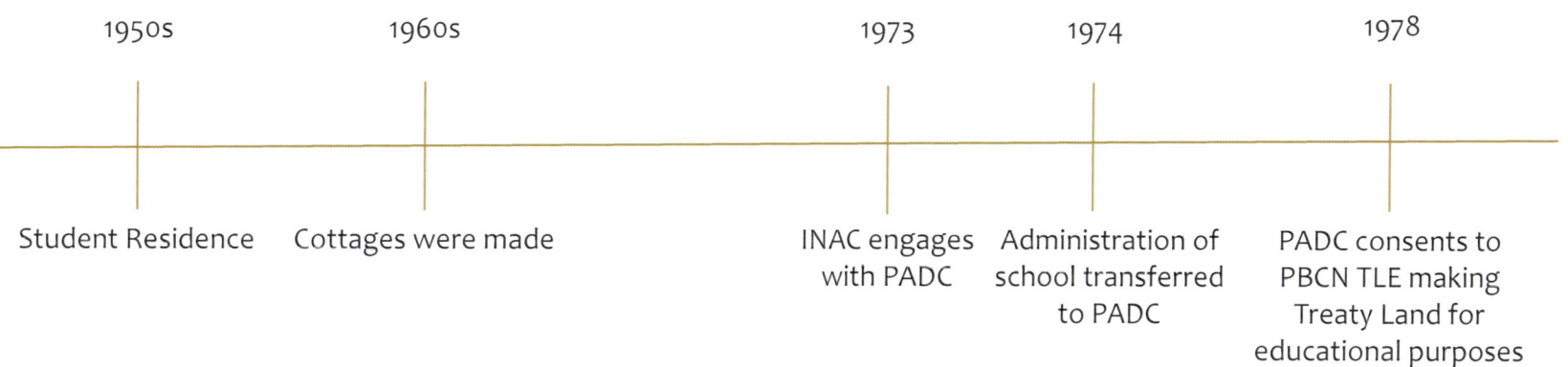

- At the end of World War 2, the federal government began operating the Prince Albert Indian Student Residence in what had been army barracks on federal crown, lands, and the Anglican church operated a school for the same process.

- In 1962, the army huts were replaced with cottages.

- In 1973, the federal government involved the Prince Albert District Chiefs in an advisory capacity and began to engage First Nations employees in the day-to-day operations of the school.

- In 1974, the administration of the school was transferred to the Prince Albert District Chiefs and funds would flow through Wahpeton Dakota First Nations.

- On or about December 13, 1978, the PADC, Council of Chiefs consented to the PBCN's TLE selection of the land commonly known as the Prince Albert Indian Student Residence, provided that when the land attained reserve status, it would be set aside under section 18 (2) of the Indian Act for educational purposes for Indian children from the member First Nations.

Lac LaRonge "All Saints" Anglican School was destroyed in 1948 due to fire and students were moved to Prince Albert.

These students were moved to a military basic training complex on the outside of Prince Albert.

Right: PA Classroom with Principal Bramwell, ca. 195-, The General Synod, Anglican Church of Canada/P7556-46

 As one author puts it, "we recognize that we need to understand the past to understand the present and where we are going in the future," (Cote-Meek, 2016, p. 32).

In 1950, one of the army buildings was renovated to accommodate 29 Gordon's Indian Residential School (IRS) students, due to water supply shortage.

With Onion Lake, LaRonge and Gordon's IRS, the Prince Albert Indian Residential School increased from 165 to 485 students, making it the largest Indian Residential School in Canada.

 Because of past colonial policies, "there is a direct relationship between the historical experience of Aboriginal peoples and the current patterns of violence in Aboriginal communities," (Cote-Meek, 2016, p. 33).

Students were housed in six H-shaped huts, two wings were joined by the bathroom and washroom areas. The remaining huts housed the eleven classrooms in which grades one to eight were taught.

Barracks

 These interrelated colonial projects are all tethered to the master colonial policy: the Indian Act, based on the greatest myth of all, the doctrine of discovery and *terra nullius*, a Latin expression meaning "no man's land," and which has been used in international and settler laws and academic theories to justify colonialization and the erasure of Indigenous sovereignty over Indigenous lands" (Brunette-Debassige, 2023, p. 40).

There was a Home Economics Room and a Manual Training Shop.

School kitchen, ca. 1935

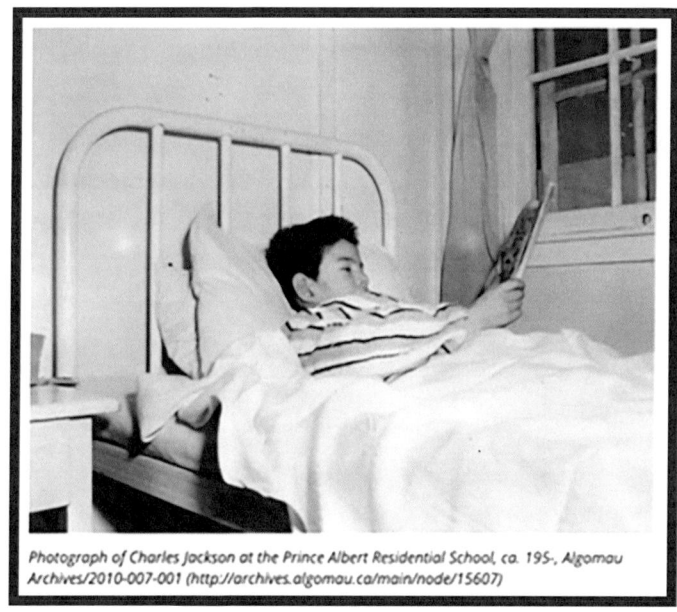

Photograph of Charles Jackson at the Prince Albert Residential School, ca. 195-, Algomau Archives/2010-007-001 (http://archives.algomau.ca/main/node/15607)

Another hut contained the staff quarters, the office and the hospital.

 While enfranchisement was an assimilation tactic presented by government as an "opportunity" to join the dominant white settler society, it involved eradicating Indigenous rights to land and eliminating the special status accorded to Indigenous peoples, thereby "getting rid of the Indian problem" and obfuscating the government's fiduciary responsibilities enshrined in Treaty agreements" Brunette-Debassige, 2023, p. 53).

The Prince Albert Residential School was considered a fire hazard for most of its history because it was overcrowded. During the 1960s, it remained a student residence as students began to enrol in municipal schools.

Girls in front of hut, ca. 1950, ACC Bernice Logan fonds/P2004-09-136

Bernice Logan taught at All Saints Residential School in Prince Albert, Saskatchewan from 1949-1952, ca. 1950, Algomau Archives

 Current researchers find that "structural racism has the ability to transcend from structural/macrolevel drivers to impact health at the individual level. These findings illuminate how structural-level factors can have micro-level influences at an individual level and can influence one's chronic disease journey and progression" (Stelkia, 2023, p. 14).

Political Change

Constitution Committee

BEGINNINGS OF THE PAGC

In the 1960s, the twelve Chiefs of the Prince Albert District formed a political alliance, to collectively work together on common issues, which was formalized under the Charter of the Federation of Saskatchewan Indians (FSI). In the early years, the Chiefs met during the FSI All Chiefs Conferences, to discuss pressing issues and to elect a District Representative, who sat on the Executive Council of the FSI, which later became known as the Federation of Saskatchewan Indian Nations (FSIN).

Initially, the Prince Albert District Chiefs (PADC) only addressed concerns of a political nature and did not employ any staff, with the exception of the fifteen employees they hired, at the beginning of the 1975/1976 school year, to operate the School Block of the Prince Albert Indian Student Residence (PAISR), which was still under the control of Indian Affairs at that time. Then, in 1982, a Convention Act was passed formalizing the organization. This was followed by the development of the administrative side of the organization, in 1984, which was incorporated as the PADC Management Company.

> Colonial assumptions have fuelled many colonial projects, including the Indian Residential School system, the boarding school system, involuntary/voluntary enfranchisement laws, the pass system, the reservation system, the ban on the Potlatch and Sun Dance, the elimination of the buffalo, Métis removal, the overlooking of Treaties, forced sterilization of Indigenous women, and military and police controls over Indigenous lives and lands, to name just a few. (Brunette-Debassige, 2023, p. 40)

Gary Wouters, Director of operations (INAC) Sask. Region

Dan Goodleaf, Regional Director General (INAC) Sask. Region

In 1974 the Prince Albert District Chiefs negotiated with Indian Northern Affairs Canada (INAC) over an allegiance where First Nations can develop their own governance and educational structures.

The Peter Ballantyne Cree Nation used its Treaty Land Entitlement and claimed the 41 acres in 1981.

"Let us put our minds together and see what kind of a life we can get for our children."
– Chief Ron Michel

 Colonization is conceptualized as having four dimensions — it concerns the land, it requires a specific structure of ideology to proceed, it is violent, and it is ongoing.

First Nations from the Prince Albert area officially took over operation and control in 1984.

Chief Roy Bird, Montreal Lake First Nations

In 1977 the twelve First Nations located in central and northern Saskatchewan established a tribal council, or political alliance, which they named the Prince Albert District Chiefs (PADC).

The alliance was later formally renamed as the Prince Albert Tribal Council (PATC), then later, Prince Albert Grand Council or "PAGC."

John Peters (Sturgeon Lake First Nations) prepared an extravagant meal for the November 22nd, 1985 celebration.

Singers from Sturgeon Lake

Royal Proclamation: Most Indigenous and legal scholars recognize the Royal Proclamation as an important first step toward the recognition of existing Aboriginal rights and title, including the right to self-determination. In this regard, the Royal Proclamation is sometimes called "the Indian Magna Carta." The Royal Proclamation set a foundation for the process of establishing treaties.

PAGC NUMBERED TREATIES[1]

Mistahimaskaw (Big Bear)
The Cree Chief was concerned with the impossible treaty conditions that seemed to ensure perpetual poverty and the destruction of his people's way of life.
(Library and Archives Canada C-001873)

Treaty Five

Treaty Five is also known as the Winnipeg Treaty. It was signed in 1875–76 by the federal government, Ojibwe peoples and the Swampy Cree of Lake Winnipeg. Treaty Five covers much of present-day central and northern Manitoba, as well as portions of Saskatchewan and Ontario. The terms of Treaty Five have had ongoing legal and socioeconomic impacts on Indigenous communities.

Treaty Six

Treaty Six was created in 1876. It is a treaty between the federal government and Indigenous peoples on the Prairies. Cree, Assiniboine and Ojibwe leaders signed the treaty. Treaty Six territory is located in Alberta and Saskatchewan.

Treaty Eight

Treaty Eight was signed on June 21, 1899 by the Crown and First Nations of the Lesser Slave Lake area. The treaty covers roughly 841,487.137 km^2 of what was formerly the North West Territories and British Columbia, and now includes northern Alberta, northwest Saskatchewan, and portions of the modern Northwest Territories and BC, making it the largest treaty by area in the history of Canada. The terms and implementation of Treaty Eight differ importantly from those of previous Numbered Treaties, with long-lasting consequences for the governance and peoples of that area.

Treaty Ten

Treaty Ten is the tenth of the eleven Numbered Treaties. It was signed in 1906–07 by the Canadian government and Indigenous peoples in northern Saskatchewan and Alberta. Treaty Ten covers nearly 220,000 km^2 of Saskatchewan and Alberta. The terms of Treaty Ten have had ongoing legal and socioeconomic impacts on Indigenous communities.

[1] Reference for the PAGC Numbered Treaties comes from The Canadian Encyclopedia. (2023). Retrieved on August 8th, 2024 from https://www.thecanadianencyclopedia.ca/en/article/treaty-5, https://www.thecanadianencyclopedia.ca/en/article/treaty-6, https://www.thecanadianencyclopedia.ca/en/article/treaty-8, and https://www.thecanadianencyclopedia.ca/en/article/treaty-10

TREATY TIMELINE

A Timeline of Events Leading to Treaties in Saskatchewan

Treaty 6 Medal courtesy of the National Archives of Canada

Red River colonists greeted by Chief Peguis in 1821. Courtesy of the National Archives of Canada

1000 AD — The Norse are said to have been the first to arrive in what is now Canada. They were followed by the Portuguese, the Spanish, and then the French and British

1497 — John Cabot claims Newfoundland for the British

1534 — Jacques Cartier arrives and claims territory for the King of France, Francis I

1539 — Francisco de Vitoria proposes that First Nations peoples own the land that they occupy

1701 — The Treaty of Great Peace is signed in Montreal by the Wabanaki, the Iroquois and the French

1763 — The *Royal Proclamation* of 7 October, 1763 recognizes First Nations lands and governments, and outlines a treaty process between the British government and First Nations

1790 — The Ontario Treaties begin in southern Ontario

1794 — The Jay Treaty allows First Nations peoples to cross the British / American border without restrictions

1817 — The Selkirk Treaty is negotiated near the Red River area of present-day southern Manitoba

1850 — The Robinson Treaties are negotiated in present-day Ontario

Prior to European contact, First Nations peoples lived throughout North America and had practised treaty-making for thousands of years.

"An Indian Encampment" Courtesy of the Glenbow Alberta Archives

Treaty Council in Manitoba Courtesy of the Glenbow Alberta Archives

> Three barriers remain to implementing the TRC's Calls to Action:
> (1) a vision among policy-makers of the "public interest" as generally excluding Indigenous peoples;
> (2) the deeply paternalistic attitudes of politicians, bureaucrats, and other policy-makers; and
> (3) the ongoing legacy and reality of structural racism" (Brunette-Debassige, 2023, p. 84).

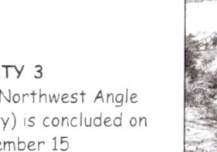

Treaty 6 negotiations in 1876. Courtesy of the Provincial Archives of Saskatchewan

Her Honour, the Lieutenant Governor of Saskatchewan, the Honourable Dr. Lynda Haverstock and Mr. Olsen with Chief Rod King of Lucky Man Cree Nation, 125th anniversary of Treaty 6, 2004 Courtesy of Fort Walsh National Historic Site

1870 — Canada purchases Ruperts land for three hundred thousand pounds (approximately $1,000,000)

1867 — The Dominion of Canada is formed. The *British North America Act* gives the Federal government jurisdiction over "Indians and lands reserved for Indians"

1871 — TREATY 1 (The Stone Fort Treaty) is concluded on August 3

1873 — TREATY 3 (The Northwest Angle Treaty) is concluded on September 15

1874 — TREATY 4 (The Qu'Appelle Treaty) is concluded September 15

1875 — TREATY 5 (The Lake Winnipeg Treaty) is concluded on September 20

1876 — TREATY 6 (Fort Carlton and Pitt Treaties) are concluded on August 23

1885 — The Riel Resistance takes place in Saskatchewan

1899 — TREATY 8 is concluded at Fond du Lac on June 21

1905 — The Province of Saskatchewan is formed

1906 — TREATY 10 is concluded at Ile-a-la-Crosse on August 28

1913 — TREATY 6 Adhesion is signed at Montreal Lake

1976 — The 100th anniversary of Treaty 6 is celebrated and renewed throughout the province

1999 — The 100th anniversary of Treaty 8 is celebrated throughout northern Alberta and Saskatchewan, including ceremonies and speeches at Fond du Lac

The 125th anniversary of Treaty 4 is held at Fort Qu'Appelle with a week-long celebration and pow wow.

2004 — The 125th anniversary of Treaty 6 is held at Fort Walsh National Historic Site in the Cypress Hills

2006 — The 100th anniversary of Treaty 10 is held 2006 in Patuanak, home of the English River First Nation

Treaty 8 Elders unveil a commemoration plaque at the 100th anniversary of Treaty 8 at Fond du Lac

The 125th anniversary of Treaty 4 at Fort Qu'Appelle

PAGC CONVENTION ACT

Within the last 50 years PAGC and their allied tribal councils formed the Federation of Saskatchewan Indian Nations.

Together with the Assembly of First Nations, they have achieved unprecedented success in the realization of social, economic, spiritual and cultural renewal for their constituents.

In 1989, the organization developed a new logo and the name was changed to the Prince Albert Tribal Council (PATC). The Chiefs of the newly formed tribal council passed a new Convention Act, in 1993, and the name of the organization was officially changed to the Prince Albert Grand Council (PAGC). The PAGC Convention is based upon the primacy and independence of each of the twelve First Nations and identifies the national, cultural and political principles that the Grand Council is founded upon and under which it is required to act. The new Convention also supports the devolution or transfer of services currently offered by PAGC to individual First Nations, as requested.

 "If we are always asking permissions to assert our culture and ways of knowing on an equal footing with other cultural world views, we thus agree to partake in our institutionalized colonization." (Cho et al., 2023, p. 84).

PRINCE ALBERT GRAND COUNCIL ORGANIZATIONAL CHART

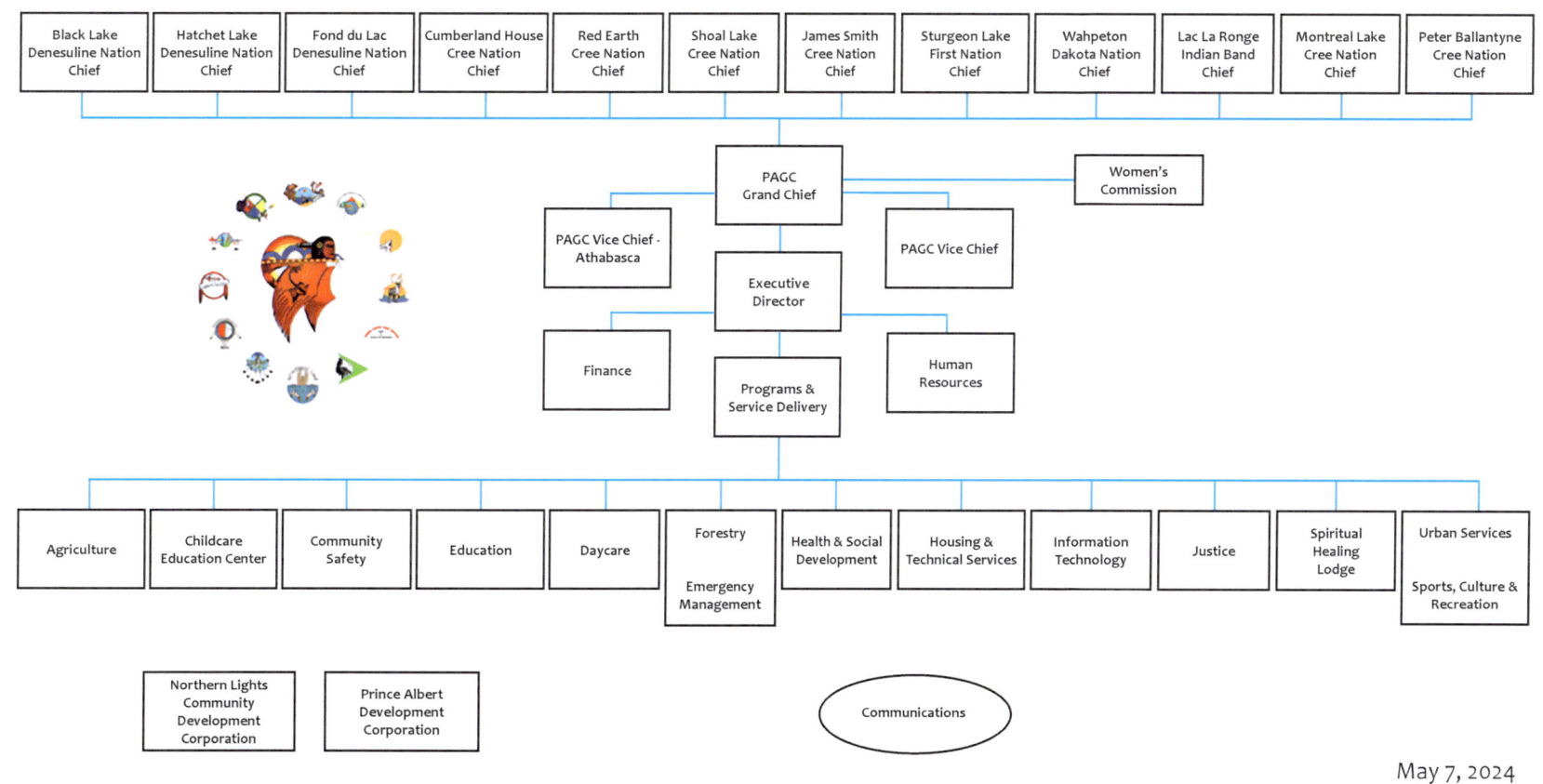

May 7, 2024

> "Indigenous faculty retention hinges on factors related to including Indigenous beliefs into the collective agreements, such as: opportunities for professional development centred on Indigeneity; the right to smudge in a personal office; inclusion in programme development; and inclusion on key administrative committees." (Cho et al., 2023, p. 94).

PRINCE ALBERT GRAND COUNCIL EXECUTIVE

Grand Chief

Brian Hardlotte was born in 1963 in Flin Flon, Manitoba to parents Rhoda and Adam Hardlotte. He was raised in Stanley Mission (LLRIB), on the trapline (little Whitemoose) where he worked at tourist and commercial fishing camps in summer. He attended the provincial school system in his community, then went to Residential School (PAISR). He graduated in 1983 in treaty band controlled system (LLRIB) Stanley Mission. He then took Forestry at SIIT. He has worked as a trapper, commercial fisher helper, exploration line cutter, mineral claim staker, geophysics, forest firefighter, crew member, crew boss, and sector line boss. He also has been an instructor teaching forest fire fighting, first aid, CPR, and GPS Mapping. His last job before going into leadership was at Prince Albert National Park in Resources. His leadership roles include (LLRIB) Education committee chairperson, (LLRIB) Band councillor (2005- fall 2010), and PAGC Vice Chief (fall 2010-2016). Since 2017, he has served as the PAGC Grand Chief.

Brian Hardlotte
Grand Chief
Prince Albert Grand Council

 Arguably, early Indigenous educators and political leaders cut a path through the deep colonial bush, thereby laying the trail for the second wave of Indigenous scholars and leaders following in their footsteps" (Brunette-Debassige, 2023, p. 54).

Vice Chief

Vice Chief Joe Tsannie is a member of the Hatchet Lake Denesuline First Nation, serving his 3rd term as Vice Chief.

The mandate of the PAGC was recently updated in the 2021 Chief's Strategic plan outlining the powers and duties of the PAGC executive. Their mandate will be designated to a team of Executive members, which according to the PAGC Chief's Act (2021);

"…provide overall direction in administration, judicial and legislative areas through the senior management of the Prince Albert Grand Council. The Senior Management Team shall include the Executive Director, The Director of Operations, the Director of Human Resources, the Director of Finance and such technical, professional or other advisors, specialists or consultants as may be considered necessary to make informed decisions," (p. 11).

Joe Tsannie
Vice-Chief
Prince Albert Grand Council

In 2016, the Liberal government responded to the TRC by publicly supporting the United Nations Declaration of the Rights of Indigenous People (UNDRIP) and removing the objector status previously enforced by the Conservative government; however, this public endorsement has yet to be fully recognized in Canadian law" (Brunette-Debassige, 2023, p. 61)

Vice Chief

Chris Jobb
Vice-Chief
Prince Albert Grand Council

Vice Chief Chris Jobb is a member of Peter Ballantyne Cree Nation, serving his 2nd term as Vice Chief.

Mission – The mission statement revised in the PAGC Chief's Strategic Plan (2015) states, "The Prince Albert Grand Council Executive will provide leadership in a comprehensive way to address issues of common concern that affect PAGC First Nation communities and its members, including Treaty protection, resource development and revenue sharing," (PPT, PAGC Chief's Strategic Plan, 2015, slide 2).

 Indigenization-reconciliation, as a system-wide process of organizational change, is intended to transform the institutions across broad areas including academics; student affairs; personnel, planning, and policy; structural development; relational strategies; and approaches and philosophies" (Brunette-Debassige, 2023, p. 69).

PRINCE ALBERT GRAND COUNCIL SENATORS

 James Burns

 Hector Kkailther

 James Stewart

 Victor Echodh

 Cy Standing

 Craig Bighead

 Roy Head

 Nolan Henderson

 Charles Whitecap

 Harry Cook

PRINCE ALBERT GRAND COUNCIL WOMEN'S COMMISSION

The Prince Albert Grand Council Women's Commission consists of 14 members from each of their respective communities. PBCN and La Ronge have two members due to their size.

The women's commission oversees the daycare and costs associated, that are high. They do fundraisers throughout year and their annual walk to bring awareness to missing and murdered aboriginal men and women.

Last year they awarded 7 scholarships at their annual banquet. With the amount of applications, it is always hard for the adjudicators to choose. Once again, they were able to do the coats, mitts, toques for those less fortunate. They also did a clothing drive and that was much appreciated with over 400 showing up.

Their efforts continue throughout the year, and the women try to help out where they can!

> The infamous "princess/squaw" binary that can be traced back to early colonists' depictions of Indigenous women. The princess stereotype tends to portray Indigenous women as good, seeking alliance with white men and institutions, and generally supportive of the settling process. The princess stereotype, however, makes Indigenous women traitors to Indigenous communities, and paints them as white and assimilated...the squaw is depicted as resisting change and standing in the way of progress. In an academic administrative context, I argue that these long-held tropes continue to mark Indigenous women's experiences" (Brunette-Debassige, 2023, pp. 93-94).

SENIOR MANAGEMENT

Executive Director

Al Ducharme, Executive Director

The Prince Albert Grand Council is a not-for-profit organization that is a political entity advocating for twelve First Nations. There are over 43,000 members that make up the PAGC making it one of the largest tribal councils in Western Canada. Since 1977, leaders of the twelve communities developed an alliance which was originally called the Prince Albert District Chiefs (PADC) which still exists today.

Vision: The Prince Albert Grand Council Executive will advocate for and assist in protecting the Inherent and Treaty Rights and Aboriginal Title of its twelve member First Nations. (PPT PAGC Chief's Strategic Plan, 2015, slide 2).

 "The Indian Act violates Article 33 of UNDRIP, which provides for the right for Indigenous peoples to determine their own identity or membership in accordance with their customs and traditions." (Luama, 2021, p. 47).

Director of Finance

Gene Der, BA, BBA
Director of Finance

Gene Der has been with the Prince Albert Grand Council for 31 years. Gene was born and raised in Meadow Lake, SK, but graduated high school in North Battleford. He received his Bachelor of Arts degree with a major in Economics in 1978 from the University of Saskatchewan. Two years after that Gene earned his business degree also at the University of Saskatchewan. After that, he attended UCLA for awhile.

 "Much of the violence experienced by Indigenous communities in Canada is cultural harm: state-sanctioned laws, policies and practices that are weaponized to assimilate, civilize and culturally erase Indigenous communities… This objective was pursued through a series of injurious State actions, including the adoption of the paternalistic and racist Indian Act, forced relocations of Indigenous communities, the operation of the Indian residential school system, forced sterilizations of indigenous women, the fostering and adoption of indigenous children in non-indigenous homes during the 'Sixties Scoop', and later through discriminatory child-welfare practices," (Luoma, 2021, p. 44).

Director of Human Resources

Karen Timmerman is a member of the Sturgeon Lake First Nation. She began working with the Prince Albert Grand Council in 1993 first as a secretary and then a Human Resource Officer. Karen has taken various classes in HR as well as leadership classes over the years. In 2019, Karen became the Director of Human Resources. Karen celebrated 30 years with the Prince Albert Grand Council in December 2023.

Karen Timmerman
Director of Human Resources

Human Resource Services are provided through several systems including:
- Recruitment and Retention
- Compensation and Benefits
- Training and Development
- Employee Relations
- Performance and Management

PAGC has over 300 employees and that number continues to grow each year by developing and establishing more programs and partnerships. Our team has continued to ensure policies and procedures were adhered to ensure best practice within our organization and to remain compliant with legislation.

 Indigenous scholars have noted their "experiences of "racial battle fatigue" (Almeida, 2015) that place additional expectations on Indigenous leaders working under White settler, patriarchal, and borderland conditions (both Indigenous and non-Indigenous environments), and that have adverse embodied impacts on Indigenous women" (Brunette-Bassige, 2023, p. 208)

Executive Office

Deanna Nelson
Executive Assistant

Deanna Nelson is a member of the Cumberland House Cree Nation. She graduated from NorPAC in 2001 with a Bachelor of Arts – Native Studies; then from S.I.I.T. in 2003 with a Business Administration Diploma. Deanna has been taking classes to continue her education in the business administration field. She started with PAGC in September 2004, and left for a short period to pursue a career in policing from May 2022 to June 2023. She realized it was not the work she wanted to be in and came back to PAGC in July 2023. In her capacity as Executive Assistant, she assists the Grand Chief and Executive Director in their schedules and arranging meetings internally and externally.

PRINCE ALBERT GRAND COUNCIL
PROGRAM MANAGERS AND DIRECTORS

Agriculture

History

Prince Albert Grand Council operates an agriculture development program in the district. There is an agrologist on staff to help plan and implement agricultural projects. This agriculture program has been servicing the needs of First Nations for close to 40 years.

Governance and Mandate

The Agriculture Program has a District Board that deals with agricultural issues and funding applications. There is a Board representative from each First Nation that contributes into the program along with a representative from the Women's Commission.

The Program's mandate includes the following objectives:

1. To promote the interest of First Nations and their membership in the agricultural industry.
2. To assist with technical information.
3. To develop viable farm business units.
4. To provide training in the different agricultural areas.
5. To assist in financial management and funding requirements.
6. To be proactive in developing new agricultural opportunities.

Betty Marleau
Program Manager of Agriculture

PAGC Agriculture

Child Care & Education Centre

Lorna Sorenson
Director of Child Care & Education Center

Leona Sorenson is a member of the Muskoday First Nation. She began working as a Child Care Worker in 1974 under the Prince Albert District Chiefs. In 1991, Leona became the Head Child Care Worker for the Prince Albert Indian Student Education Centre (PAISEC). PAISEC closed down in 1997 and in the fall of 1997 it opened up as the Prince Albert Grand Council – Child Care & Education Centre; Leona became the Co- Director in 2001. PAGC CCEC was restructured in 2019 and Leona became the Director, she remains in this position.

The PAGC has established the Child Care and Education Centre on the Chief Joseph Custer Reserve #201 in Prince Albert to serve male/female infants/toddlers/child/youth in the 18 months – 15 years of age range who are in the need of therapeutic treatment.

The Child Care and Education Centre will operate under the terms and conditions of a Service Agreement between the respective Child Care and Education Centre and the Indian Child & Family Services and/or Ministry of Social Services.

The programs for the Child Care and Education Centre will meet or exceed the standards set by the Saskatchewan Ministry of Social Services, including annual Fire, Health and Building Inspections.

CHILD CARE- There are five cottages for the children's accommodation/temporary home. We provide care and supervision in a safe, nurturing and structured environment. Each cottage has a House mother that provides home-cooked meals and nutritional snacks. The staff consists of 5 Cottage Case Managers, 40 Childcare Workers, 4 Shift Supervisors and 6 Security on the premises.

PAGC Child Care & Education Centre

Louise Nadeau is a member of the Peter Ballantyne Cree Nation. She is the youngest born to Thomas and Ethel Morin from Denare Beach (Beaver Lake). She began working with the Prince Albert Tribal Council in 1994 in the Engineering & Technical Services Department as a receptionist. Louise then became the Executive Secretary from 1998 to 2005 at the Main Office. Moving on to Health & Social Development from 2006 – 2013. In 2013, she transferred to the Child Care & Education Centre becoming the Assistant Director in 2021. Louise will be celebrating her 30 years with the Prince Albert Grand Council in July 2024.

Prince Albert Grand Council Child Care and Education Centre provides integrated therapeutic childcare and educational programming for, infants, toddlers, children and youth. It is under the governance and control of the Prince Albert Grand Council. The Centre's program can care for children who require therapeutic care, diagnostic assessment, behavioural stabilization, and transitional support toward independent living.

Louise Nadeau
Associate Director of
Child Care & Education Center

Every Child Has….

- The Right to Be Respected
- The Right to Dream
- The Right to Be Loved and Cared for
- Gifts That Should Be Recognized and Valued
- The Right to Achieve Their Full Potential
- The Right to Be Loved Unconditionally

Education Department

Edward Mirasty is a Cree member of the Lac La Ronge Indian Band and has been involved in education for over thirty years. He has worked at the Prince Albert Grand Council as Director of Education for over fourteen years, focusing on K-12 education. Before that role, he worked as Director and Principal at Sturgeon Lake First Nations and as teacher and vice-principal at his community of Little Red Reserve. Through his work, he has gathered extensive experience and has worked with various programs, including K-12 Education, Active Measures, Sports, Culture and Recreation, Child Welfare, Tribal Policing and now Homelessness.

Edward Mirasty, Ph.D. (ABD)
Director of Education

Vince Brittain is a James Smith Cree Nation Band member who grew up and attended Bernard Constant Community School. He has been married to his wife, Connie, for over twenty-four years. They have two boys. The eldest, Merit, has completed two years at the University of Regina in Social Work and has entered his fourth year of Education through the First Nations University of Canada. His youngest, Merik, has completed his first year at the First Nations University of Canada in Education. Vince has been involved in education for over 27 years and is finishing his last year of a Doctor of Education at the University of Saskatchewan.

Vince Brittain, Ed.D. (ABD) Third-Level Services Specialist

Vince believes in honesty, integrity, and trustworthiness, which leads to solid relationships. Vince's parents believed in education and strongly supported him in his educational journey. They would be proud of him as he continues his academic journey and helps empower communities as they move forward.

What We Do

The PAGC Education has continued to evolve following the Education Transformation initiative. Since First Nations have assumed their own second-level services, the department has stepped away from its second-level service delivery with a new focus of the PAGC Education third level services. For instance, the office is creating proposals for various third-level services including Self-Administered Policing, Indigenous Community Corrections Initiative, Jordan's Principle, and Northern Lights Community Development Corporation. The department has also partnered with Sask Ministry, LEADS, and Saskatchewan Teacher's Federation in providing training on Intergenerational Trauma and Resiliency Training for various professions and trades-training programs.

Many educational resources have been created that speak to the experiences of the Residential School experience, along with a curriculum developed that describes the neuro-science behind intergenerational trauma specifically for teachers and administrators. The PAGC Education office has also developed Cree, Dene, and Dakota books for grade 5-12 students as part of the Indigenous Languages Act. Most recently, the PAGC Education office has been working with Dr. Rose Roberts on Woodland Cree Myths and Legends. This pilot project is the beginning of a series of books for future sectors to collect their local stories with Elders and community members. Aside from collecting stories, legends and myths, the PAGC Education Department has also been involved with developing the Education and Community Safety Portal.

Currently, the office is creating proposals for other national programs that positively respond to Indigenous housing and homelessness concerns. Both staff members are currently completing their Ph.D. and Doctorate of Education degrees with a focus on decolonization strategies for educational institutions. Through an Indigenous lens, they can provide professional training, such as Education Board Training, Team Building Activities, Technology and Education, Environmental Scan of Education Ecosystems, Policy Development, and introduction to the Danielson Framework for teachers, principals and administrators.

PAGC Education

Forestry and Emergency Protective Services

Cliff Buettner
Director of Forestry and Emergency Protective Services

The Director provides staff direction, personal development and financial administration for all staff and acts as an agent with all 12 First Nation communities for delivery of the Saskatchewan Public Safety Agency Long-Term Service Agreement and other community projects. Additional responsibilities are delegated to Michelle Vandevord, Associate Director, to include leadership for all staff under Saskatchewan First Nations Emergency Management and Search and Rescue.

The Forestry and Emergency Protective Services program provides Response Service contract administration for 36 First Nation sustained action fire crews in our 12 First Nations as part of a Saskatchewan Response Service Agreement. Additionally, Saskatchewan First Nations Emergency Management and PAGC Search and Rescue and Recovery SARSAV Chapter for all Saskatchewan First Nations are administered through our office.

We provide Wildland Fire Certification Training through contractual Services with the Saskatchewan Public Safety Agency. We concentrate on Education, Prevention and Mitigation and have completed many on-reserve Fuel Hazard Reduction Projects funded through Indigenous Services Canada and Mitigation contracts tendered through the Saskatchewan Public Safety Agency under the Disaster Mitigation Adaptation Fund.

The PAGC Wildfire Resilience Initiative is currently documenting Indigenous Wildland Fire knowledge to successfully build relationships across institutions and communities to facilitate intergenerational knowledge sharing. This has established First Nations community protection and habitat restoration through Cultural burning and have developed a website (**wearefire.ca**) as a toolkit for indigenous led fire practices being recognized and accepted nationally.

wearefire.ca

Michelle Vandevord
Associate Director of Forestry and
Emergency Protective Services

My name is Michelle Vandevord (Day Star Woman) from Muskoday First Nation, Saskatchewan, where I have resided for over 25 years. I'm a mother of three daughters and three sons. I'm also a very proud Kokum to four grandsons. I started volunteering to be a good role model for my daughters and females in my community. It is also to keep my grandmother's and mother's volunteer legacy alive in my family. I 'am the longest-serving female firefighter and the first female Captain in my fire department's history. I'm very proud to be a part of a very active and progressive First Nation Volunteer Fire Department. I have received our Fire Departments Hubert Bear Memorial Award for volunteering which I'm very proud of as it is named after my uncle. I was honored by my community when I received the Fire Service Exemplary Service Medal with my brothers in the pow wow circle. I am the Associate Director for Saskatchewan First Nation Emergency Management (SFNEM) in Prince Albert.

SFNEM has two delivery arms which are Firefighting and Emergency Management. We provide free Firefighting and Emergency Management training to all Indigenous communities. We also respond to emergencies when requested to our communities. The Prince Albert Grand Council Search, Rescue and Recovery team is made up of SFNEM employees.

We have the most advanced underwater drone equipment and are leaders in this field of search and rescue. Our team is a member of the Saskatchewan Search Rescue and Association of Volunteers (SARSAV) which means we respond to searches across the province when requested. As an organization we are always adapting to the needs of our communities. My team is improving fire and emergency services on reserve and I'm proud of our success.

Forestry and Emergency Protective Services

- Saskatchewan Public Safety Agency
- Firesmart
- Muskrats to Moose
- Disaster Mitigation Adaptation Fund
- Wildfire Resilience Initiative
- Prince Albert Model Forest
- PAGC Search and Rescue
- SK First Nations Emergency Management
- Emergency Management Training and Services
- Fire Fighting Training and Services
- Community Fire Safety Enhancement Program
- Fire Prevention Presentations

PAGC Forestry
& Emergency
Protective Services

Health and Social Development

Above: Shirley Woods, BSN, MPH, Director of Health

Shirley Woods is originally from the Muskeg Lake Cree Nation and has worked at the Prince Albert Grand Council for 10 years, 5 of those in nursing and the last five as Director of Health and Social development. She has a Bachelor of Science in Nursing from the University of Saskatchewan and a Master of Public Health from the University of Washington. Her nursing career has spanned over 40 years in a variety of roles, including working in Northern Saskatchewan, Nursing supervisor, Nurse epidemiologist and an educator. Twenty-nine of these years has been working with First Nations in transferred communities. She is a strong advocate for preventative health care and supporting our communities to improve health outcomes.

PAGC Health & Social Development

Vision: Empowering communities, families and individuals to achieve and maintain holistic health.

Mission: In the spirit and intent of our inherent Treaty Right to Health, and in partnership with our First Nations, Prince Albert Grand Council Health and Social Development supports the delivery of safe holistic community health and wellness programs.

The Prince Albert Grand Council's Department of Health and Social Development provides health and social programming and services to our 12-member First Nations. The programs provided may vary in each community depending on funding agreements and the community's needs. Our department continues to display excellence and innovation through best practices in health care. In 2024, PAGC Health and Social Development achieved Accreditation with commendation through Accreditation Canada. The accreditation process has supported us on our journey of continual quality improvement. Treaties are a foundation for our health care programs and services at PAGC. The health environment has shifted from an exclusive federal Treaty-based premise to a collaborative inter-jurisdictional approach. We continue to protect and promote our Treaty rights while building partnerships with external health and social agencies.

Penny Constant
Associate Director of Health

Penny Constant is a mother of 5 and a proud kokum of two handsome grandsons. She is a James Smith Band member who brings numerous years of community health management to the Prince Albert Grand Council (PAGC). Her career in health management began in James Smith upon the completion of the Health Coordinators Training program from the University of Regina (SIFC) and thereafter became the community's first trained health coordinator and the transfer of health services was expanding. She remained in her home community for fourteen years and played an integral role in the design, implementation, and delivery of community health services. Penny has been with PAGC for fifteen years as the Associate Director of Health and during this time became a certified Health Manager through the First Nations Health Managers Association. She attributes much of her success to the many great role models and leaders who share the same passion for improved health and well-being for the many people and communities of PAGC.

Regular engagement, participation, and feedback from the PAGC's Health Directors Working Group, Health Commission Chiefs, and Women's Commission is evidence of our collaboration with the communities. In our partnership with the Victoria Hospital expansion, we have been instrumental in the design, model of care and workforce planning.

PAGC's Department of Health and Social Development provides programs and services based on a holistic health and wellness model. Programs directly run or facilitated are: Public Health, Home and Community Care, Primary Care (Hatchet Lake Denesuline Nation) nursing, Diabetes Education and Support, Dietitian services, Tobacco Control, Dental Therapy, Medical Reprocessing Facility, Maternal Child Health, HeadStart and Daycare, Environmental Health, Indian Residential Schools (IRS) Resolution Support Treaties serve as a foundation for our health care programs and services at PAGC.

The health environment has shifted from an exclusive federal Treaty-based premise to a collaborative inter-jurisdictional approach. We continue to protect and promote our Treaty rights while building partnerships with external health and social agencies.

Housing and Technical Services

Frank Bighead, Director of Housing & Technical Services

Frank Bighead, Director, Prince Albert Grand Council (PAGC) Housing & Technical Services and has been employed by PAGC for 45 years. He is a fluent Cree Speaker from Sturgeon Lake First Nations. Also, he is a Founding Member of First Nation National Building Officer's Association (FNNBOA). He sits on various boards including the Saskatchewan First Nation Housing Liaison Committee. Educational background includes: Interprovincial Journeyman Carpenter, Building Official – Class 1, Fire Investigations, Fire Prevention and Inspections, 3rd Class Power Engineer (SK), Building Operator "A" (AB), Systems Maintenance Management (SAIT, SIIT), Basic Plumbing Inspections, Wood Energy Technical Transfer, HRAI Suite of Workshops Ventilation Trainer. Frank is responsible for management, direction, administration, and implementation of activities for First Nations in regard to Housing and Technical Services.

Rosie Charles is a member of the Lac La Ronge Indian Band and has been involved in First Nation Housing for twenty-nine years working in different capacities. She has been with Housing and Technical Service for eight years and worked 11 years for her home community, consulting and facilitating with various First Nations across Canada, she worked with the federal government in effective and efficient housing practices in Administration, Project Management, Band Construction and Property Management. She is the founding board member and holds her designation with the First Nations Housing Professional Association.

Rosie Charles, Associate Director of Housing & Technical Services

History

The Engineering and Technical Services Program started in 1983 when Prince Albert Grand Council was given funding to do Fire & Housing Compliance to PAGC twelve First Nations. The personnel hired to do this function were the Late Raymond Standing of Wahpeton Dakota First Nation, Leland McCallum of Peter Ballantyne Cree Nation, and Napoleon Mercredi of Fond Du Lac Denesuline Nation. In 1984, Henry Felix of Sturgeon Lake First Nation was hired as a Housing & Fire Safety Inspector. The department has grown over the years as technical services were devolved from Indian Affairs & Health Canada to Tribal Councils.

PAGC Technical Services consists of fifteen (15) full time employees in various areas of specialization and who are dedicated to improving the infrastructure and living conditions in the thirty two communities of our twelve First Nation members.

Housing & Technical Services looks after **Housing, Community Planning and Capital, Information Systems** and **Maintenance Management**.

Housing

Conducts Capital and CMHC Program inspections for new housing and rehabilitation projects including:
- Plans evaluations
- Site inspections
- Prior to backfill, Foundation inspections
- Prior to drywall, framing, insulation & vapour barrier
- Final inspections

Conducts code compliance inspections & plan evaluations for:
- CMHC Section 95 new housing & rehabilitation projects
- Daycare and Head-Start structures
- Indian Child and Family Services structures
- Teacherages, Nursing Residence and other small buildings

Provides and administers the PAGC Better Building Approval System "BBAS" including:
- Providing Housing Bylaw template(s)
- Managing and maintaining PAGC's code plus housing specifications.
- Adhering to the latest versions of the Canadian Model Construction Codes & Standards
- Providing building approvals (aka building permits) including occupancy certificates
- Providing technical advice on engineering, construction and building design issues.
- NOTE: PAGC Housing Services maintains a small library of basic house plans that can be modified to suit. (1 to 5 bedrooms including duplex to four-plex floor plans)

Provide a Housing Circuit Rider Trainer Program
- Conduct housing program assessments, identify strengths and weaknesses
- Compile information into a strategic plan complete with one-on-one training and mentorship working toward the development of a manageable Housing Program.
- Coordinate and conduct training of First Nations Housing Coordinators & Staff
- Provide assistance and advisory services on housing programs including policy development, proposal development, cost estimating, procurement practices and assist with housing authority development.

Community Planning and Capital

- Coordinates community land use and infrastructure plans with 5-year planning updates.
- Assists in capital planning and funding negotiations.
- Participates in project teams for major capital projects.
- Provides project management on selected projects.
- Provides training in contracting and project management to First Nations members.
- Advises and assists in contracting and engineering services.
- Conducts surveys and community mapping.

Information Systems

- Maintains an inventory of community facilities and assets through the Capital Asset Inventory System (CAIS) and housing databases, updated yearly.
- Coordinates Asset Condition Reporting System (ACRS) with 5-year updates.
- Updates Capital Management Data Base (CMDB) yearly.
- Provides technical support to capital projects and management.
- Updates housing maps.
- Developing a Geographic Information System (GIS).
- Conducts Global Positioning System (GPS) surveying.
- Provides computer-assisted drafting and design services.

Maintenance Management

- Advises in the maintenance of water/sewer and building systems.
- Responds to emergency repair services requests.
- Maintains computerized Maintenance Management System (MMS) including records of maintenance and equipment inventories for each community.
- Provides training and advice to First Nations maintenance staff.
- Conducts new Home Owner's Workshops.
- Provides Building Systems Maintenance Training.
- Health Centre maintenance program.
- Infrastructure Training

PAGC Housing & Technical Services

Human Resources

PAGC Jobs

Ruth Jobb is a member of the Peter Ballantyne Cree Nation from Southend Reindeer Lake. She graduated from S.I.I.T. in 1994 with a Business Administration diploma. Ruth has been in continual education, attending and taking various courses and workshops. She has gathered a wide range of experiences in the field throughout the years. She has been with Prince Albert Grand Council for 29 years in various positions in the human resources department.

Ruth Jobb, Associate Director of Human Resources

The PAGC Human Resource Team has remained diligent in recruiting and retaining employees while giving preference to PAGC First Nations' members.

The PAGC Human Resource Team consists of Karen Timmerman (Human Resource Director), Ruth Jobb (Associate Director), Cristy Leavey (Human Resource Clerk), and Melanie Constant (Executive Administrative Assistant).

This team of four (4) work to support our employees, who in turn provide service excellence to our twelve (12) First nations.

Our team continues to work on standardizing and updating HR Processes and policies to ensure we are in line with current labour standards and best workplace practices.

We are continually meeting with various program to ensure that we remain competitive in the workforce by conducting regular reviews of our salary grids to maintain our staff and remain competitive in the workforce.

Information Technology

Mike Wells, Director, Prince Albert Grand Council (PAGC) Information Technology Services has been employed by PAGC for 21 years. His education and experience in Computer Science and various Computer Service centres gave him the skills to cover all aspects of information technology.

He started with PAGC as an application developer in which he built multiple websites and applications still in use today, such as the PAGC website and the human resource information system. After five years, Mike took on the director position. As director, he is responsible for the management, direction, administration, and implementation of various information technology solutions for PAGC departments and First Nations.

Along with his team of highly skilled staff, he is constantly researching and testing the ever-evolving technology field for possible advances in efficiency and productivity for PAGC and its First Nations.

Mike Wells, Director of IT Services

Department Goals

- Continually improve and adapt to new technologies
- Set a standard of support that communities can look to
- Provide evolving proof of concepts to First Nations (consulting, development)
- Promote collaboration and partnerships
- Cultural preservation and expansion
- Provide digital independence and sovereignty

PAGC Information Technology

Justice Unit

I was born and raised in Prince George BC. I moved with my family to my father's home reserve (James Smith Cree Nation) when I was about 12 years of age. I went to school in Kinistino, Saskatchewan.

I joined the RCMP in 1984, and I served in the RCMP until I retired in 2006. During that time I was stationed in North Battleford, Sandy Bay, Indian Head and the was in charge of the Carry The Kettle satellite office which we assisted in transitioning into the first Saskatchewan First Nations Police Force known as the File Hills Police Service.

I developed the First Nations Cadet Corps in 1996 while stationed at the Carry the Kettle First Nations with the assistance and guidance of Elder Wilma Kennedy, a retired school teacher and Elder Andrew Ryder, a military veteran.

The program content continued to expand and after one year had seen a decrease in Youth Crime of 31% and an increase in Academic performance of 19%. In the following years, more communities joined on across Canada where I had trained cadet instructors, which eventually evolved into the Community Cadet Corps.

I was promoted in 1999 to the Corporal rank in the Aboriginal Policing Section of the RCMP overseeing policing and contract policing in Saskatchewan First Nations.

In 2010 I became Director of Justice for PAGC in 2010, and still teach cadets to this day with a PA Urban and Sturgeon Lake First Nations Cadet Corps.

Rick Sanderson
Program Manager of Justice Unit

Justice is healing "to enhance and support the provision of justice services and develop new initiatives in a culturally sensitive manner, recognizing the importance of utilizing First Nations methods to heal both the individuals and communities within the Prince Albert Grand Council region and surrounding areas, while adhering to the Spirit and intent of the Treaties".

Types of programming provided are:
- Victim/Offender Mediation
- Accountability Hearing
- Formal Cautioning Agreements
- Family Group Conferencing
- Healing & Talking and Sentencing Circles
- Community Justice Forums

We continue to see an increase of files being diverted from the Courts to our program, and we maintain constant contact with the Crown and the Police to encourage more files to be directed to the program to be dealt with.

It is encouraging to see more jurisdictions going the Pre-Charge route with Alternative Measures instead of tying up our already stressed court system.

When called upon the Justice Unit mediators can assist in diffusing situations before they become a matter for the police and courts through mediation. This includes situations in the home, schools and workplaces.

The First Nations Cadet Corps is not only designed to keep youth out of trouble and out of our court system, but to encourage and prepare for the future in which we may need future officers for Self Administered policing which is presently sought by PAGC and some First Nations.

The Justice Unit oversees the following programs:
- Rural Community Justice Program
- First Nations Cadet Corps
- Prince Albert Urban Alternative Measures Program
- Saskatchewan Aboriginal Court Worker Program

PAGC Justice Unit

Men's Spiritual Healing Lodge

Carol Connoly, BISW Program Manager
Men's Spiritual Healing Lodge

PAGC Spiritual
Healing Lodge

Biographical Information

Carol Connolly is a member of Muskeg Lake Cree Nation and has been involved in Justice for over twenty years. She began her career with the Prince Albert Grand Council in 2007 as the Alternative Measures Program Coordinator and, in 2008, she took on the position as the Justice Director. In 2013/2014, she was pivotal in the reopening of the Spiritual Healing Lodge where she became the manager.

About the program at the Men's Spiritual Healing Lodge

We provide 24-hour security for federal offenders and through rehabilitation, we assist in providing culture, spirituality, and traditions from Elders from the four sectors of PAGC.

We assist in providing services and benefits that CSC cannot itself provide or cannot provide to an Aboriginal offender in a cost-effective or culturally sensitive manner, which will assist the Aboriginal offender to become a law-abiding citizen; and assist to facilitate the development of skills on accessing the broader Aboriginal social and community services network that support the reintegration of an offender, who would benefit from these specialized services.

Spruce Lodge Boarding Home

Corrine Fiddler, Program Manager of Spruce Lodge Boarding Home

Corrine Fiddler is member of the Muskeg Lake Cree Nation. Originally beginning with a practicum placement at the PAGC Justice Unit back in 1999 she would move on to different positions within the Grand Council. She took on the role of Program Manager for Sprucelodge Boarding Home in 2010 and she remains today.

Spruce Lodge Boarding Home is a medically approved home that provides meals, accommodations and transportation to registered First Nations clients who come to Prince Albert to access medical services that are not available in their home community. The program is funded by Health Canada and as such, follows the Non-Insured Health Benefits Policy Framework. Spruce Lodge currently employs 8 full time and 5 casual staff delivering four distinct programs.

There are four separate programs being delivered by Spruce Lodge:

1. In-City Transportation assists clients that "reside in" Prince Albert and have been referred to a specialist not available in the city.
2. Medical Transportation assists clients arriving from "outside" of Prince Albert who have appointments in the city.
3. After Hours Call Centre assists registered Treaty clients who require assistance outside of regular working hours. This scope is across all of Saskatchewan.
4. Mental Health Benefit assists registered treaty individuals and communities with assistance to access and/or approve mental health support services where needed.

Spruce Lodge has undergone a great deal of changes in the recent years, but none as significant as our move to our new permanent location at 150-34th Street West. Our new facility is a joint venture between the PAGC and the Hatchet Lake Band who collaborated to purchase the former Days Inn building and turn it into our new Spruce Lodge Medical Boarding Home.

Our facility is currently undergoing renovations that will provide a brand new commercial kitchen and a large gathering lounge for our guests to comfortably visit or simply await their transportation back to their communities.

PAGC Spruce Lodge Boarding Home

URBAN SERVICES

Geoff Despins is the Director of PAGC Urban Services and is a member of the Lac La Ronge Indian Band. He joined the Prince Albert Grand Council – Urban Services in 2002 as a Youth Employment Coordinator. Over his 22 years, he served in various positions as a Labourer Force Development Coordinator and Partnership Coordinator before taking the position as the Director of PAGC – Urban Services.

Within the city of Prince Albert and PAGC Communities, our mandate is to research, develop, implement, and promote employability, and reduce the criminal rate and criminal behaviour. Our programs are designed specifically to encourage positive and healthy family dynamics by providing the necessary resources and support to families. We also provide education to inform and promote traffic safety. Through partnerships with Sask Lotteries, our office engages our youth by highlighting programming in the Sports, Culture and Recreation area.

Geoff Despins
Program Manager of Urban Services

Urban Services oversees the following:
- Urban Services Labourer Forces Development (SITAG)
- Athabasca Labourer Forces Development (SITAG)
- Safety Coordinator (SGI)
- Reintegration Coordinator (CSC)
- Sports, Cultural and Recreation (Sask Lotteries)
- Outreach Van
- Vulnerable Housing Coordinator (River Bank Development)
- CPAC (Community Action Plan for Children)

PAGC Urban Services

PRINCE ALBERT GRAND COUNCIL COMMUNITIES

Wahpeton Dakota Nation

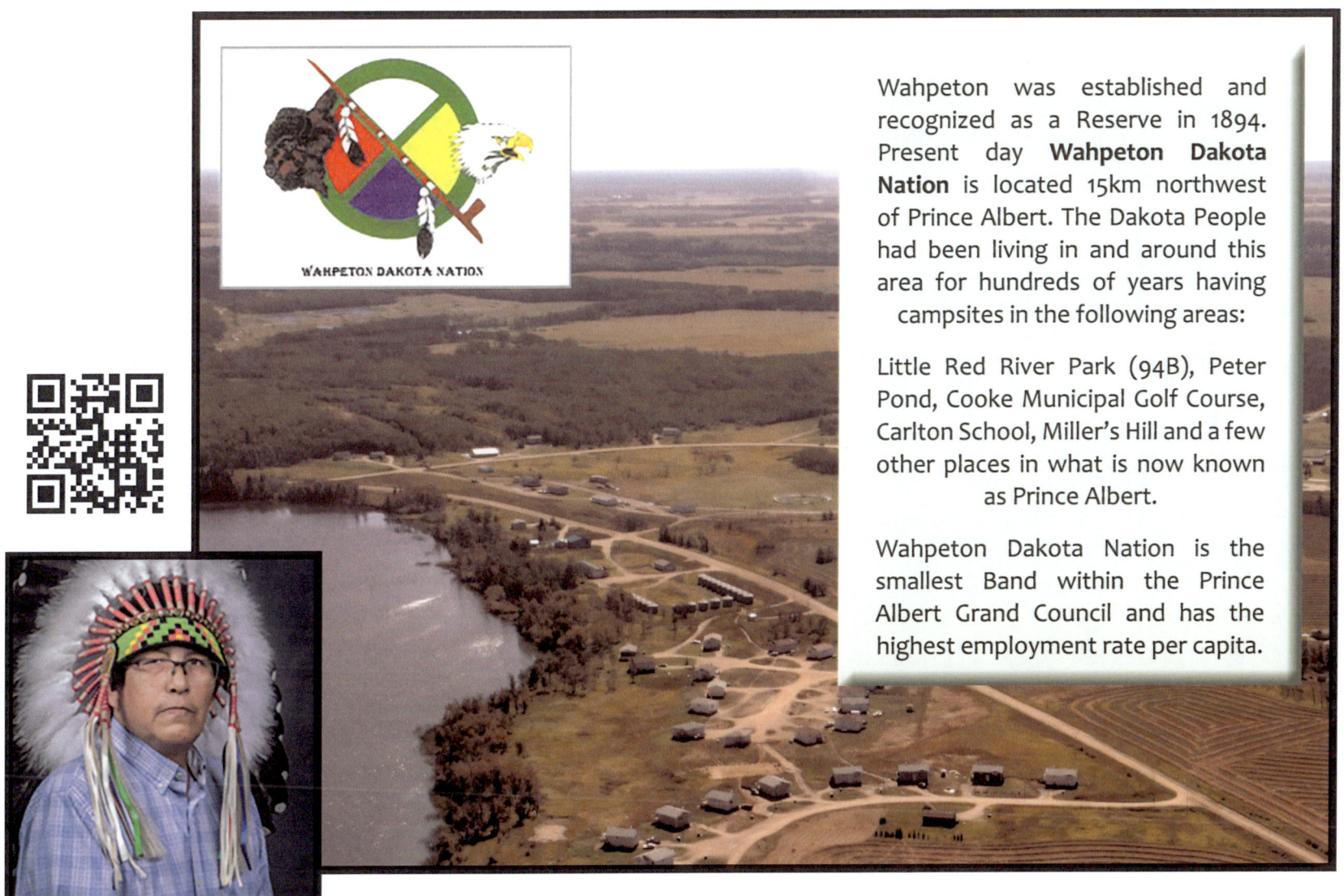

Wahpeton was established and recognized as a Reserve in 1894. Present day **Wahpeton Dakota Nation** is located 15km northwest of Prince Albert. The Dakota People had been living in and around this area for hundreds of years having campsites in the following areas:

Little Red River Park (94B), Peter Pond, Cooke Municipal Golf Course, Carlton School, Miller's Hill and a few other places in what is now known as Prince Albert.

Wahpeton Dakota Nation is the smallest Band within the Prince Albert Grand Council and has the highest employment rate per capita.

Chief John Waditaka

Shoal Lake Cree Nation

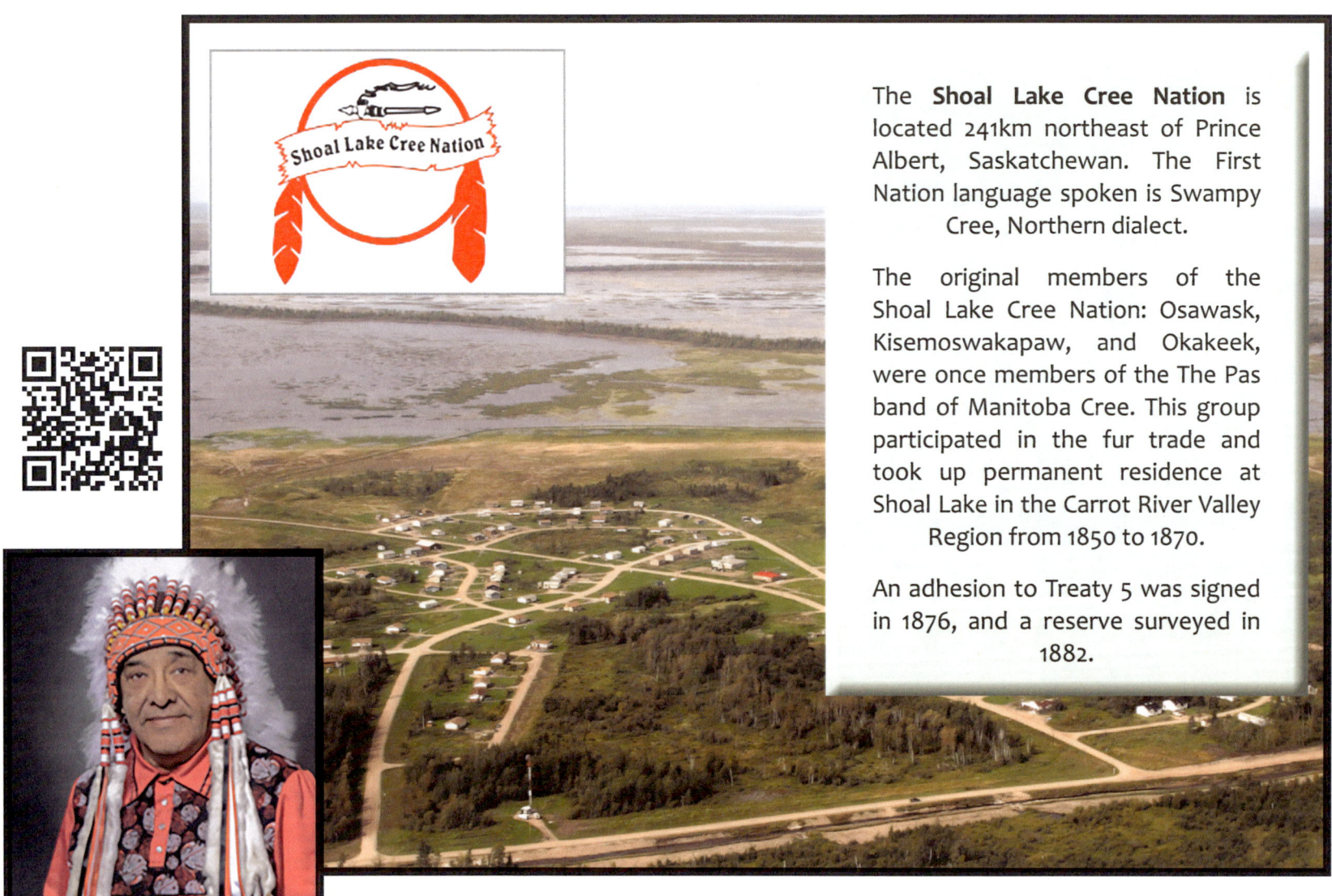

The **Shoal Lake Cree Nation** is located 241km northeast of Prince Albert, Saskatchewan. The First Nation language spoken is Swampy Cree, Northern dialect.

The original members of the Shoal Lake Cree Nation: Osawask, Kisemoswakapaw, and Okakeek, were once members of the The Pas band of Manitoba Cree. This group participated in the fur trade and took up permanent residence at Shoal Lake in the Carrot River Valley Region from 1850 to 1870.

An adhesion to Treaty 5 was signed in 1876, and a reserve surveyed in 1882.

Chief Marcel Head

Sturgeon Lake First Nation

Sturgeon Lake Reserves 101 and 101A are located 55 kilometres northwest of the City of Prince Albert. The two reserves are in the Forest Fringe area of Saskatchewan.

The members of **Sturgeon Lake First Nation** are descended from Cree Chief Ah-yah-tus-kum-ik-im-am and his four headmen (Oo-sahm-us-koo-nee-kik, Yay-yah-too-way, Loo-sou-am-ee-kwakn, and Nees-way-yak-ee-nah-koos) who signed Treaty Six near Fort Carlton on August 23, 1876.

The Band was first listed as William Twatt Band, in reference to the Chief's English name, then in 1963, changed to the Sturgeon Lake Band, and now is known as the Sturgeon Lake First Nation.

Chief Christine Longjohn

Black Lake Denēsuline First Nation

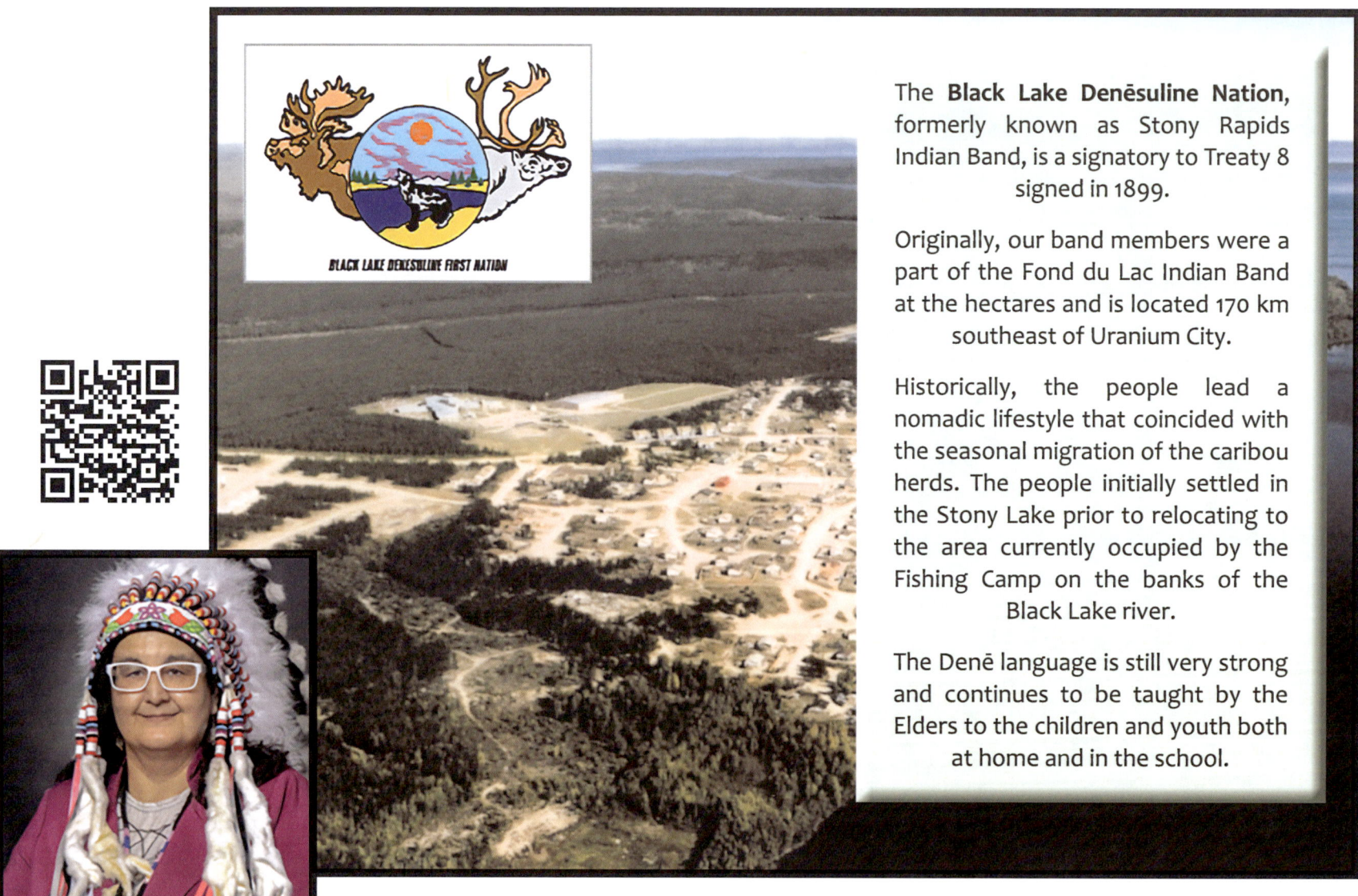

The **Black Lake Denēsuline Nation**, formerly known as Stony Rapids Indian Band, is a signatory to Treaty 8 signed in 1899.

Originally, our band members were a part of the Fond du Lac Indian Band at the hectares and is located 170 km southeast of Uranium City.

Historically, the people lead a nomadic lifestyle that coincided with the seasonal migration of the caribou herds. The people initially settled in the Stony Lake prior to relocating to the area currently occupied by the Fishing Camp on the banks of the Black Lake river.

The Denē language is still very strong and continues to be taught by the Elders to the children and youth both at home and in the school.

Chief Coreen Sayazie

Lac La Ronge Indian Band

The Lac La Ronge Indian Band (LLRIB) is a progressive Woodland Cree First Nation located in the majestic boreal forest in north-central Saskatchewan.

The Lac La Ronge Indian Band is a multi-community Band and is the largest First Nation in the province. The central office is located on the Kitsaki reserve adjacent to the Town of La Ronge.

Chief Tammy Cook-Searson

Peter Ballantyne Cree Nation

The **Peter Ballantyne Cree Nation** has a total of seven communities noted as follows:

- Pelican Narrows
- Kimasom Pwatinak (Deschambeault Lake)
- Wapaskokinow (Sandy Bay)
- Denare Beach (Beaver Lake)
- Southend
- Kinasao
- Sturgeon Landing

The First Nation language spoken is Woodland Cree. This band signed Treaty 6 on February 11, 1889.

Chief Peter A. Beatty

Cumberland House Cree Nation

The **Cumberland House Cree Nation**, formerly known as the Cumberland House Band, signed an adhesion to Treaty 5 on September 24, 1875 at Norway House along with the Saulteaux and Swampy Cree tribes.

There are a total of five designated reservation lands that make up the Cumberland House Cree Nation. These five reservation lands are:

Pine Bluff
Muskeg
Cumberland 100A
Budd's Point
Cumberland Reserve 20A

The main reservation was Pine Bluff and there were a total of 75 members who were transferred and relocated from Pine Bluff to the current location of Cumberland Reserve 20A next to the Village of Cumberland House, in September of 1964.

Chief Rene Chaboyer

Fond du Lac Denēsuline First Nation

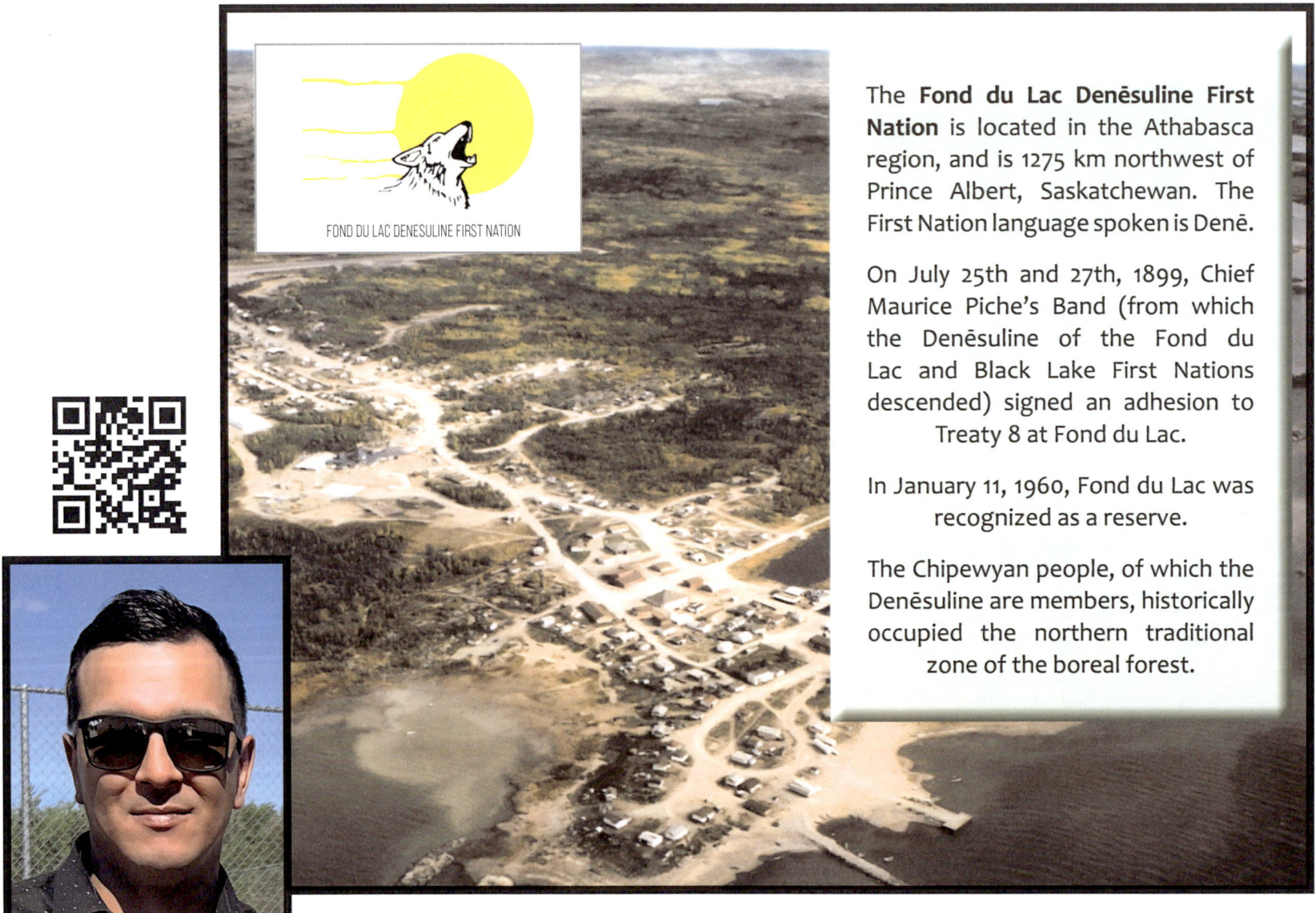

The **Fond du Lac Denēsuline First Nation** is located in the Athabasca region, and is 1275 km northwest of Prince Albert, Saskatchewan. The First Nation language spoken is Denē.

On July 25th and 27th, 1899, Chief Maurice Piche's Band (from which the Denēsuline of the Fond du Lac and Black Lake First Nations descended) signed an adhesion to Treaty 8 at Fond du Lac.

In January 11, 1960, Fond du Lac was recognized as a reserve.

The Chipewyan people, of which the Denēsuline are members, historically occupied the northern traditional zone of the boreal forest.

Chief Ronnie A. Augier

James Smith Cree Nation

The **James Smith Reserve** was historically known as Fort-a-la-Corne. Situated near the banks of the North Saskatchewan River, Fort-a-la-Corne became a gathering place of many different First Nations.

Later this area would become a gateway to the western regions of Canada. Trading posts would eventually become a common place with the Hudson Bay Company and Northwest Trading Company, as both French and English traders competed for the economic benefits of the fur trade.

Along with the fur trade came the inevitable settlement of the Europeans around the fertile lands we occupied. They founded their homesteads, built churches, schools, and supply centres, trading with the surrounding Indian peoples.

Chief Kirby Constant

Montreal Lake Cree Nation

Montreal Lake Cree Nation are members of the Woodland Cree. They signed adhesion to Treaty 6 in 1889, and were formerly known as the William Charles Band. Currently, it is comprised of two communities, number 106 and 106B, which includes the Little Red Reserve.

Through oral teachings, our Elders continue to speak of the historic occupation and traditional use of the lands within the Prince Albert National Park region. A nomadic people, the Montreal Lake Cree Nation made use of the land through traditional life sustaining practices such as hunting, trapping, fishing, the gathering of berries and medicines, shelter and participating in spiritual and ceremonial gatherings.

Chief Joyce Naytowhow-McLeod

Hatchet Lake Denēsuline First Nation

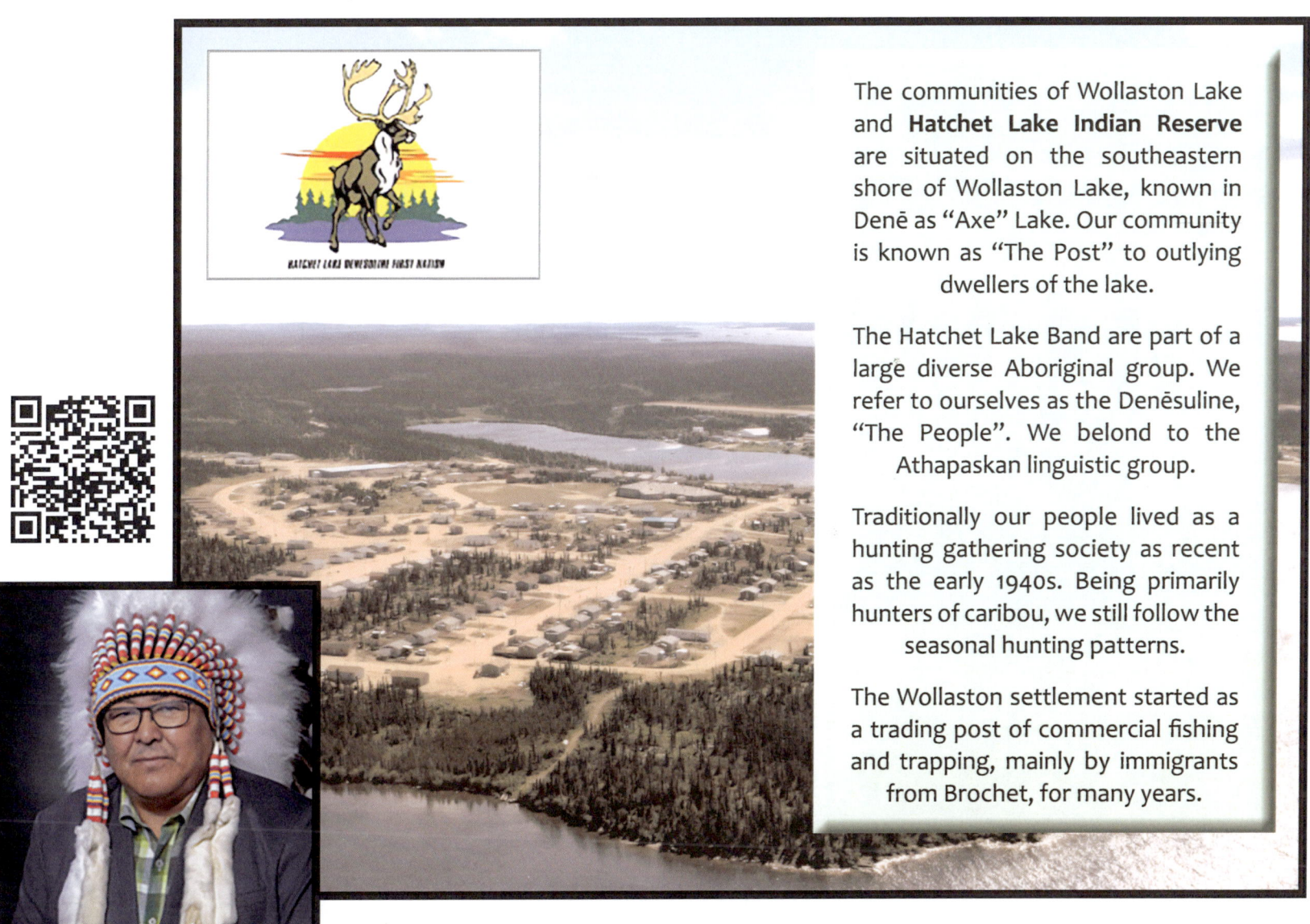

The communities of Wollaston Lake and **Hatchet Lake Indian Reserve** are situated on the southeastern shore of Wollaston Lake, known in Denē as "Axe" Lake. Our community is known as "The Post" to outlying dwellers of the lake.

The Hatchet Lake Band are part of a large diverse Aboriginal group. We refer to ourselves as the Denēsuline, "The People". We belond to the Athapaskan linguistic group.

Traditionally our people lived as a hunting gathering society as recent as the early 1940s. Being primarily hunters of caribou, we still follow the seasonal hunting patterns.

The Wollaston settlement started as a trading post of commercial fishing and trapping, mainly by immigrants from Brochet, for many years.

Chief Bartholemew J. Tsannie

Red Earth Cree Nation

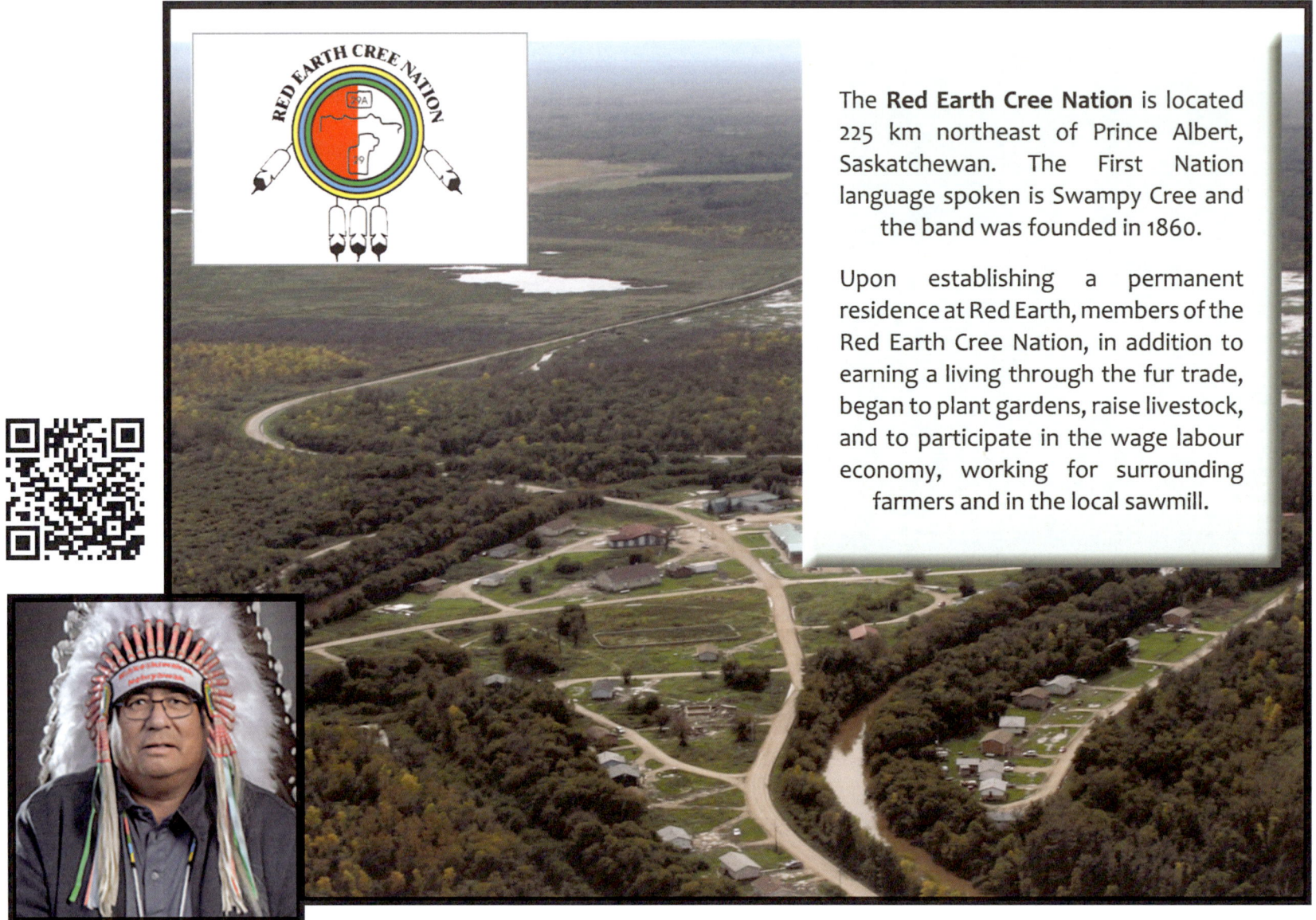

The **Red Earth Cree Nation** is located 225 km northeast of Prince Albert, Saskatchewan. The First Nation language spoken is Swampy Cree and the band was founded in 1860.

Upon establishing a permanent residence at Red Earth, members of the Red Earth Cree Nation, in addition to earning a living through the fur trade, began to plant gardens, raise livestock, and to participate in the wage labour economy, working for surrounding farmers and in the local sawmill.

Chief Zachary Whitecap

HELP LINE FOR RESIDENTIAL SCHOOL SURVIVORS

Provided by: Government of Canada - Indigenous Services Canada and Crown-Indigenous Relations and Northern Affairs Canada

National Indian Residential School Crisis Line

1-866-925-4419

The National Indian Residential Schools Crisis Line exists to provide support for former Residential School students. The Crisis Line provides:

- Emotional and crisis referral services
- Information on how to get other health supports from the Government of Canada Cultural support
- Emotional support
- Professional counseling
- Transportation
- Accessing health support
- Coping with emotional reactions

SPECIAL THANKS

Tina Pelletier, Photographer,
Indigenous Creature Communications

The PAGC gives thanks to Tina Pelletier of **Indigenous Creature Communications** for providing many of the photos of our Program Directors and Managers used in this book.

Since November 2022, Indigenous Creature Communications has carved out a niche in crafting messages that deeply resonate within First Nations communities across Saskatchewan. At its helm is Tina Pelletier, a proud member of Pasqua First Nation and a direct descendant of Chief Pasqua who was one of the original signatories of Treaty #4. Tina also holds a deep connection to the Métis community of Ste. Madelaine, located in Manitoba.

With an academic background in Journalism and Indigenous Studies, including a Masters in Intercultural and International Communication, coupled with 25+ years of hands-on experience in the communications field -- including 10+ years at the Prince Albert Grand Council -- Tina is a powerhouse in her own right.

As an advocate and visual storyteller, Tina's vision goes beyond standard communications. She is well-versed in the nuances of Indigenous issues and governance, employing her research and analytical skills to navigate politically sensitive topics. Her mission is to provide a platform for Indigenous leaders to be heard, to amplify their voices by creating and implementing marketing and communication strategies that reverberate with the target audience. This mission goes beyond simply providing services—it cultivates relationships, builds bridges, and promotes understanding.

From advocacy communications to media relations and photography, her diverse services are all linked by a common goal: shaping the future of First Nations communication, both as a solo endeavour as well as a collaborator with local creative talent.

Her commitment to her clients is as steadfast as her support for community leaders in times of crisis. Tina's photography services complement her communication offerings, providing professional visuals for corporate, event, and lifestyle needs.

For thoughtful communication and compelling visual narratives, Tina Pelletier is the specialist who ensures your story not only matters but stands out.

To learn more about Tina and her services contact her at indigenouscreaturecomms@gmail.com or 306-941-7120.

BIBLIOGRAPHY

Brunette-Debassige, C. (2023). Tricky Grounds: Indigenous Women's Experiences in Canadian University Administration. Regina, Saskatchewan: University of Regina Press.

Cho, C. Corkett, J.K., Steele, A. (Eds.).(2018). *Exploring the toxicity of lateral violence and microaggressions: Poison in the Water Cooler.* North Bay, ON: Palgrave Macmillan.

Cote-Meek, S. (2016). *Colonized Classrooms.* Fernwood Publishing. Kindle Edition.

Davenport, C. (2022). Here's what we know about Gordon's Residential School. Retrieved on Oct. 26, 2023 from https://regina.ctvnews.ca/here-s-what-we-know-about-gordon-s-indian-residentialschool-1.5870309.

Government of Canada. (2024). *250th Anniversary of the Royal Proclamation of 1763 Hilliard55! HH.* Retrieved from https://www.rcaanc-cirnac.gc.ca/eng/1370355181092/1607905122267.

Luoma, C. (2021). Closing the cultural rights gap in transitional justice: Developments from Canada's National Inquiry into Missing and Murdered Indigenous Women and Girls. *Netherlands Quarterly of Human Rights.* Vol. 39(1), pp.-30–52.

Office of the Treaty Commissioner. (2024). *Treaty Timeline.* Retrieved from www.otc.ca/resource/category/maps.html.

Steckley, John L & Bryan D. Cummins, *Full Circle, Canada's First Nations.* Toronto: Pearson Prentice Hall, 2008. 122.

University of Regina. (2023). Prince Albert (All Saints) Indian Residential School. Retrieved on Oct. 28, 2023 from https://www2.uregina.ca/education/saskindianresidentialschools/prince-albert-indianresidential-school/.

www.ingramcontent.com/pod-product-compliance
Lightning Source LLC
Chambersburg PA
CBRC100812010526
44107CB00023B/1270